ONLY

BEDS

Editor-in-Chief
ALEJANDRO ASENSIO

Subeditor and texts
EVA MARÍN

Art Editor
MIREIA FABREGAS

Editorial Staff
ROBERTA VELLINI
XAVIER ROSELLO
CARLOS RIVERO

Photographic Documentation
SEAN ROVIRA
ASTRID MARTEEN
DANIEL JARAMILLO

Production Director
JUANJO RODRÍGUEZ NOVEL

Design and Layout
MANEL PERET
JORDI CALLEJA

Infographics
TONI LLADÓ FERNÁNDEZ
ENRIC NAVARRO
MANEL PERET

Traduction
MARK HOLLOWAY
MARGARIDA RIBEIRO
DAVID SUTCLIFFE

Copyright © 2004 Atrium Group
Published by:
Atrium Group de ediciones y publicaciones S.L.
Ganduxer, 112
08022 Barcelona

Tel: +34 932 540 099
Fax: +34 932 118 139
e-mail: atrium@atriumgroup.org
www.atriumbooks.com

ISBN: 84-96099-52-0
D.L.: B-50.164-2004

Printed in Spain
Ferré Olsina S.A.

INDEX

Metal
148

Fabrics
174

Day beds
244

Introduction

Long gone are those medieval times in which the bed was one of the most highly valued possessions of the home and, as a consequence, was handed down from father to son. Throughout history, the bed has been used for a great diversity of functions. Richard III traveled on it to the battlefield and to his death. It was when he died that it was discovered that he had used it to store his riches in and that for this reason it had been so difficult to transport. In the French court of the 17th century, or in the palaces of the Renaissance, it was the place favored for receiving visitors while, for the women of the old Rumanian countryside, it was the ideal place for kneading the dough for their bread. Matisse painted some of his masterpieces on it while the writers Onetti or Mark Twain found some of their greatest inspiration while lying on this piece of furniture. It was as of 1945 that the change started to take place in this sector. The bed ceased to be a static element made of noble materials and started to adapt to and reflect the lifestyle of its owners. However, the real revolution has come about over the last few years thanks to the application of the new technologies. Computerized and electronic designs have appeared which allow us to remain active from the bed along with versatile designs conceived for the ever-changing flexible society of today which demands something more than a piece of furniture to sleep on. It demands something to live on that does not sacrifice aesthetics for functionality. On the following pages, we will see beds that can be set in different positions, beds with tables incorporated, with built-in storage space, with pockets for magazines and so on, beds from which to watch television and in which to read, round beds, beds for living designed by the best creators from the international panorama.

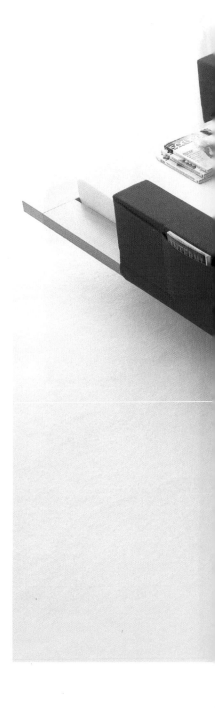

leather

Leather is one of the richest materials and one which produces one of the most sophisticated effects in a particular ambience. In the following, we will see beds into which leather has been incorporated into some of their elements or even to upholster the complete structure. The latest tendencies in beds of this type introduce colors in ochres and orange tones along with rounded forms with an air of the 1970's. In this chapter, models with a great diversity of appearances have been selected. Some appear to be trivial, of a greatly reduced expression, with thin legs and slim bedheads while others have been given a great presence with pronounced volumes and seem to be anchored to the floor. There are also those that play with geometry and allow for a broadening of their functions to different uses. This may be achieved by the incorporation of elements such as cushions that can be situated by the bedhead or anywhere else to serve as an auxiliary table or as a small backrest so that you can read or work in a half lying position on the mattress. And, although this may be with an informal or more exotic air, the use of leather always leads to elegance. On occasions, this elegance may come close to luxury and be complemented with a profusion of details such as cushions in rich fabrics or other types of tanned hides which explores the possibilities of different textures to the maximum or even in a more austere nature in a way in which a few well-chosen components stand out.

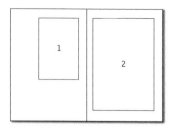

1. Detail of the Thur headboard, from the LEMA company.
2. CASADESÚS CYCSA bring us the Laturka bed (above) and the Alma bed (below).

PATRICIA URQUIOLA

Patricia Urquiola was born in Oviedo (Spain) and she now lives and works in Milan. She assisted Achille Castiglione and Eugenio Bettinelli with the courses that they presented in the Polytechnic Institute of Milan and in the ENSCI in Paris from 1990 to 1992. Later, she started to work for De Padova in the development of new products. She associated with Vico Magestretti and set up a studio. In 1996, she started directing the Lissoni Associati design group for Cappellini, Cassina, Kartell, Artelano y Antares-Flos among others. At the same time, she designed independently for Moroso, Fasem, Livi't, Tronconi and Bosa. She participated in "Abitare il Tempo" from 1998 to 2000 and her products were selected for the Italian Design 2001. She presently has her own studio in Milan and she dedicates her time to design, exhibitions, art direction and architecture.

Profile

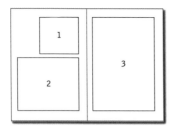

1. Sandi Renko has designed this model for FRAUFLEX.

2. The Dox model from FORMER.

3. Alfa comes from the Emaf Progetti studio, and is available from ZANOTTA. the headboard and the pouf are upholstered in polyurethane /Du Pont Dacron, and the structure is steel. The outside cover is removable. In some versions, the posture can be adjusted manually or electronically.

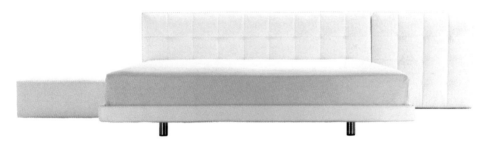

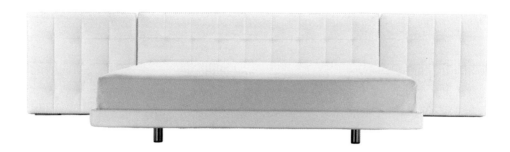

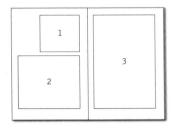

1. CATTELAN ITALIA features this model by Paolo Cattelan in its catalogue: Maui.

2. A model from CANTORI.

3. R. Barbieri is the designer of Lietto, distributed by ZANOTTA.

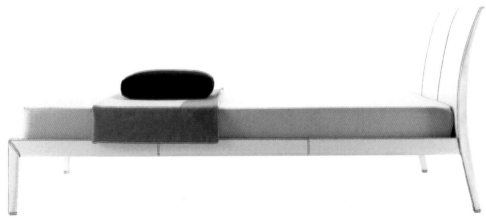

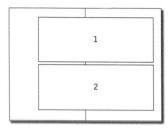

1. Asia (left) and Royal (right) are two products from BONALDO, designed by Stefano Cavazzana.

2. Two versions of the Vulcano model from the FLOU company, created by Rodolfo Dordoni.

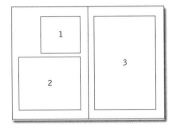

1. Giuseppe Viganò has created Skyline for BONALDO.

2. This bed is manufactured by FLOU, and designed by Rodolfo Dordoni: Duetto.

3. A CATTELAN ITALIA bed, upholstered in leather, with chrome steel legs - created by Emanuele Zenere: Kawai.

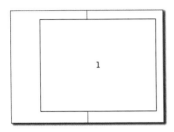

1. Various FRAUFLEX models, created by designer Sandi Renko.

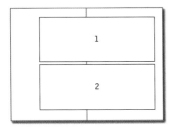

1. Another model from FRAU-
FLEX.

2. MÖLLER DESIGN present this
design by Cord Möller-Ewerbeck:
Marvin.

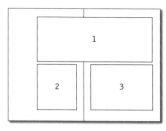

1. MINOTTI produce Bartlett Letto, designed by Gordon Guillaumier.

2. POLIFORM present this model with a headboard that can be lowered.

3. Cité is from MOLTENI & C, and created by Paola Navone.

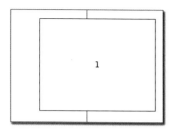

1. Paolo Piva created this model,
   Smara, for WITTMANN.

PAOLA NAVONE

This designer has demonstrated his skills in an extensive range of activities. After graduating at Turin Polytechnic in 1973, he acted as assessor of image to various governmental agencies in Southeast Asia for which he worked on development, image and quality products in design and furniture. At the beginning of the 1980's, he collaborated, closely, with the technicians at Alessi's. The enthusiasm of both parts materialized in the Collection of trays "Mizar". He later set up the company Mondo with Giulio Capellini and in 1986, he became art director of Orizzonti. Paola Navone has also designed installations that show his impeccable sense of the theatrical.

Profile

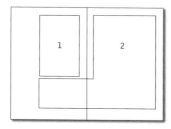

1. PHILIPP PLEIN include this model in their atalogue.

2. You and me (above) and Glamour (below) are two beds produced by IVANO REDAELLI.

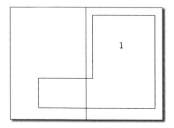

1. An idea from POLTRONA FRAU,
   the Lullaby Due model designed
   by Luigi Massoni & 967.

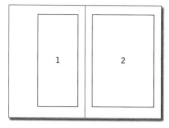

1. Kelly (above) and Égoiste (below) are two models from PHI-
LIPP PLEIN.

2. Rodolfo Dordoni created Party
for FLOU.

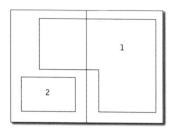

1. Plan (left) and Double Bed (overleaf) have been created by Piero
   Lissoni for MATTEOGRASSI.

2. MATTEOGRASSI feature this
   design by Franco Poli in their catalogue: Openside.

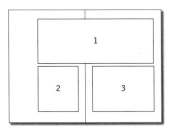

1. The Plan model, designed by Piero Lissoni for MAT-TEOGRASSI.

2. AUPING present the Royal Day Bed, a creation by Thomas Al-thaus.

3. Another creation by Piero Lissoni produced by MATTEOGRASSI.

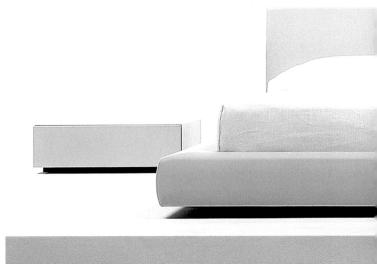

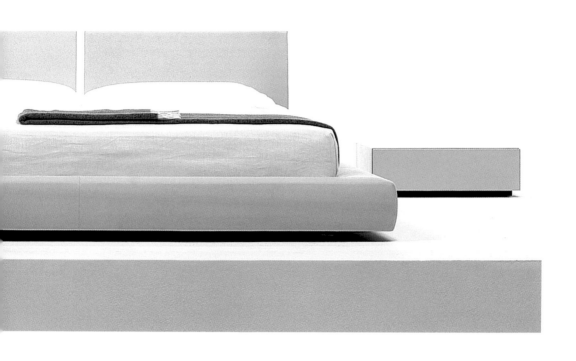

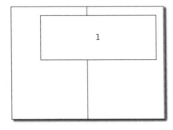

1. Various models from PRESOT-
   TO.

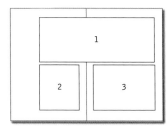

1. Franco Poli created Openside for the MATTEOGRASSI company.
2. A bed from IVANO REDAELLI.
3. This bed combines wengue and leather, sold by CLUB8COMPANY.

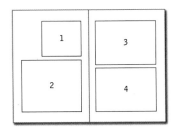

1. BONALDO present Skyline by Giuseppe Viganò.

2. The MÖLLER DESIGN product range includes this creation by Cord Möller-Ewerbeck Marvin.

3. Peter Ross has designed Max for BONALDO.

4. Bes is from GIORGETTI's Al-trove collection

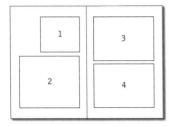

1. A design from VERARDO.
2. Geo is a bed in the GALLI catalogue.
3. The Papillon model from LUNA.
4. Jean is produced by IPE CAVAL-
   LI, designed by Roberto Lazzeroni.

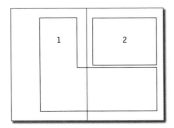

1. IPE CAVALLI present their model Round Trip, from its Cavalli Night collection.

2. Also from IPE CAVALLI, Big Sleep, designed by R. Lazzeroni.

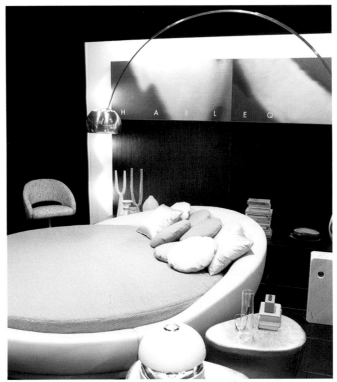

wood

Wood has been one of the materials most used to produce beds since this piece of furniture came into being. Since its origins, the bed has changed as much as society itself and now it could be said "tell me how you sleep and I'll tell you what you are" as how you sleep has become a reflection of the lifestyle of your dreams. On the following pages, we will find designs that range from beds with the smallest of bases, on which to place the mattress and which respond to the oriental philosophy of sleeping in contact with the ground for the most mystical, to the most sophisticated versions that go far beyond a piece of furniture on which to rest and incorporate other elements of furnishing such as shelves, drawers and cupboards or even accessories such as lights for the most demanding. For the nostalgic there are models with high bedheads, which are given classical elegance by rich woods, and, in contrast, there are other lower ones finished in colored-lacquers or upholstered in fabrics that make them more suitable for young or informal spaces. In general terms, the designs of today shun excess and overloading, but play with details that enrich the surfaces with different textures and reliefs. Another feature of the contemporary bed is its versatility and, in the following, we will see models that incorporate backrests, large strategically situated cushions and other elements in order to convert the bed into another space for activity.

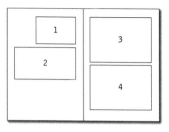

1. Yang, from LAGO.
2. RAFEMAR present the Mimo model.
3. INTERI bring us this model by designer Gabriel Teixidó: Ele.
4. A model from the MOBILIFICIO PREALPI company.

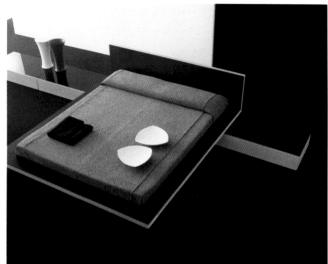

RODOLFO DORDONI

Rodolfo Dordoni was born in Milan in 1954. He graduated in architecture at the Polytechnic University of Milan in 1979. After various experiences in different architectural studios, he started working in the area of industrial design. He worked on strategies of image ranging from those for products to those of the communication sectors. From 1979 to 1989, he took on the responsibilities of the artistic direction and coordinated the image for Cappellini. He has practiced as a consultant and designer for different companies apart from his activity as architect and designer of commercial establishments, stands and pavilions.

Rodolfo Dordoni has collaborated with Acerbis, Arteluce, Artemide, Moroso, Tisenttanta, Driade, Venini, Flos, Fontana Arte, Lema, Fiam, Foscarini, Minotti, Dolce & Gabbana, Molteni, De Sede, Halifax, and Flou among others.

Profile

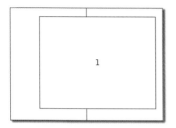

1. A very versatile bed from LAGO.

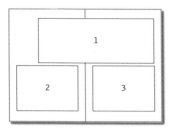

1. AZCUE bring us this model: Programa Blok, from the studio of Abad Diseño.

2. Serie 0 + 1, designed by F. Poli for BERNINI.

3. Another Yang design from the LAGO company.

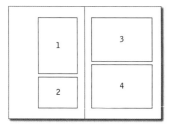

1. Quatro is a bedroom from OR-GANICA-ON.

2. Rodolfo Dordoni has created the Salina model for FLOU.

3. Tadao, by Vico Magistretti, is another creation from the FLOU company.

4. Another design by Vico Magistretti, available from FLOU.

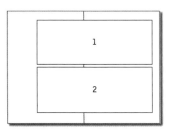

1. Ave created by Abad Diseño, for AZCUE.

2. A bed in the Sistema Notte range, designed by Piero Lissoni for CAPPELLINI, a series of modules to create different compositions for the bedroom area.

3. Ponte is a LUNA product.

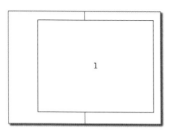

1. Soberb is a model designed by Héctor Diego. It forms a part of a collection of timeless bedrooms with geometric lines - combining ultra shine finishes, wood: oak, mongoy or wengue.

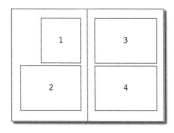

1. Yoshida is a bed from the EM-MEBI company.

2. BERNINI feature this bedroom with its straight lines in the 0 + 1 series.

3. The Piana model from LEMA.

4. Another version of the Soberb model, designed by Héctor Diego.

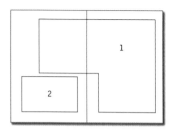

1. Bed with canopy by William Sawaya. SAWAYA & MORONI are the manufacturers of this model, Liorah.

2. Another model from SAWAYA & MORONI, Sospir, created by Toni Cordero.

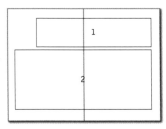

1. The PORRO company feature this model, created by Piero Lissoni: Garden.

2. Two canopy beds from the BIS BIS company.

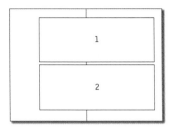

1. Afra and Tobia Scarpa have designed Morna for MOLTENI & C.
2. Diamond is a creation by Patricia Urquiola, produced by MOLTENI & C.

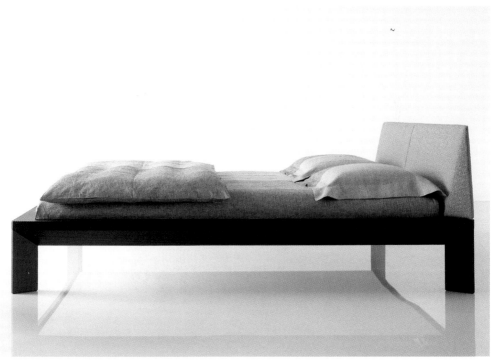

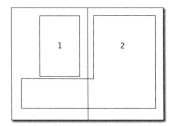

1. The Bomber Model from ELITE.
2. Three models from INTERI, created by designer Gabriel Teixidó.

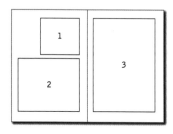

1. Kobe, designed by Vico Magistret-ti is a bed in lathe-turned solid beech with a mattress which can be taken apart. From DE PADO-VA.

2. PROMEMORIA offer this Romeo Sozzi creation.

3. Two models from OSTER: Atena (above) and Meran (below).

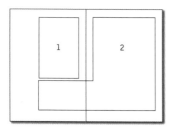

1. HORM present this creation by Carlo Cumini, Nos Al.

2. Soho (on this page and overleaf, top) and Lady (bottom) from VE-RARDO.

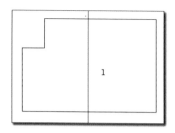

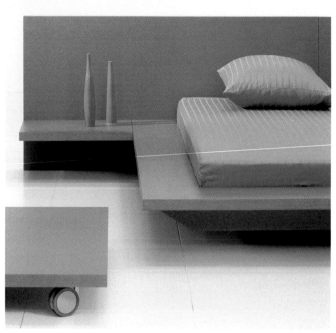

1. The JUVENTA company present:
   Pi.

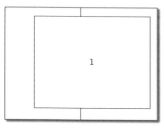

1. Different details of the Aton bedroom, from the house of KLENK.

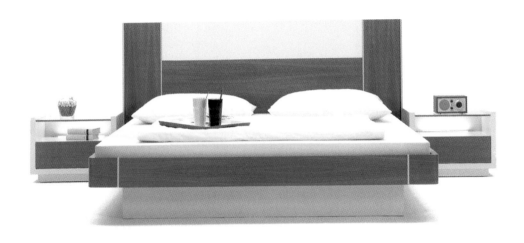

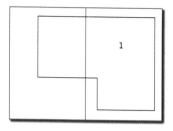

1. Raratong is a design from the
   KLENK catalogue.

ANTONIO CITTERIO

Antonio Citterio (1959) has demonstrated that he has talent in a number of different disciplines. His experience covers a diversity of fields: architecture, interior design, corporate design, industrial design... The furniture of this Italian designer shows the admiration that he feels for minimalist art. As much his architectural creations as his furniture design are characterized by their functionality and they stand out for their essential forms which are able to transmit a lot with very few elements. In order to achieve this expressive simplicity, the quality of the materials used becomes basic. Citterio states that he only designs pieces of furniture that he would like to be surrounded by. His creations can be found in the permanent exhibitions of the MOMA (Museum of Modern Art of New York), the Pompidou Center in Paris and the Museum of Architecture and Design of Chicago.

Profile

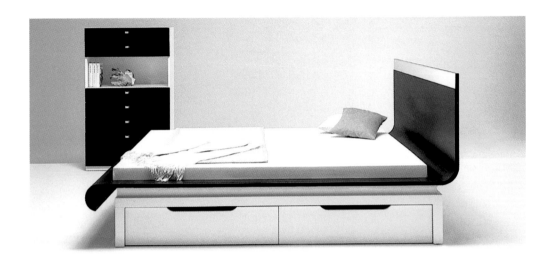

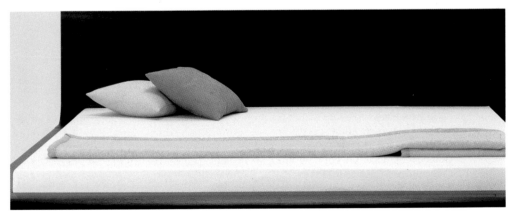

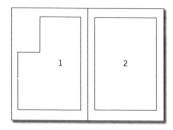

1. ZEIT RAUM present their model, Silence.

2. The AUPING brand produce Auronde, designed by Frans De La Haye (above), and Royal (below) by Thomas Althaus, which has individual adjustment of the angle, among other features.

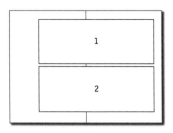

1. Antonello Mosca has designed Hermitage for the GIORGETTI company.

2. BIS BIS present this model with its minimalist statement.

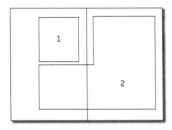

1. This design by Paola Navone, Cité, is available from MOLTENI&C. The frame is wooden (wengue, natural oak or grey oak), or alternatively, fabric, velvet or leather lined. The model illustrated here has a plush headboard. Can be completely removed for washing.

2. Three models produced by the BIS BIS company.

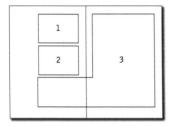

1. The Vegas model from NOLTE.

2. OSTER manufactures this model

3. Other models produced by the NOLTE company: Prima (below), and overleaf, Salto (top) and Tampa (bottom).

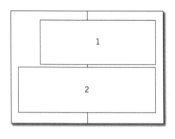

1. Soberb: a design by Héctor Diego.

2. Extra Bed, a creation by Baron & Baron for CAPPELLINI.

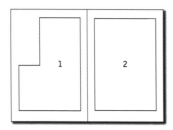

1. RUHE RAUM's Ravena model, available in different types of wood, can be combined with different bedside tables.

2. Two designs from GERVA-SIONI's Otto collection.

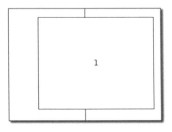

1. Various GERVASONI models with Zen lines.

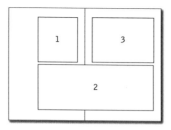

1. The Aton's headboard can be extended to the bedside tables. Available from KLENK.

2. FORMER present Plano, by Pinuccio Borgonovo (left) and Rond, by Luigi Vaghi (right).

3. Detail of the headboard and bedside table of a model from GERVASO, in harmony with Zen precepts.

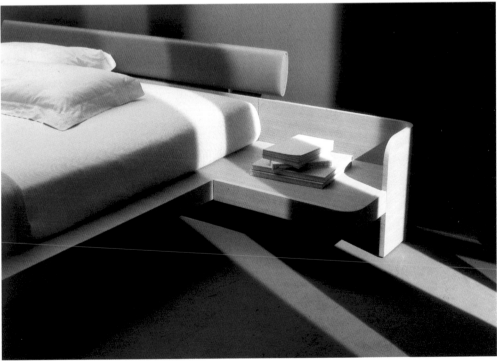

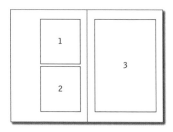

1. Altera is featured in ZALF's catalogue.

2. Presenting DI LIDDO&PEREGO'sDomino model.

3. Monopoli in two different combinations, from the ZALF company.

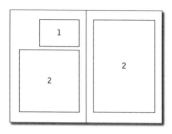

1. The Domino model from DI LID-DO&PEREGO.

2. ZALF present Oh! Razio Dynamic (this page) and two combinations of Castello Di Lot (overleaf).

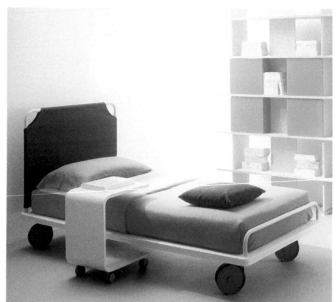

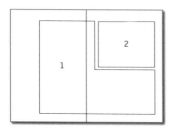

1. Two versions of Castello Di Lot (this page top, and overleaf, bottom) from ZALF, permitting different combinations. Benefit (bottom) is another design from the same company.

2. DI LIDDO&PEREGO's Domino model.

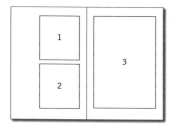

1. CLUB8COMPANY feature this model in their catalogue.

2. Classic is a versatile model from LUNA.

3. These two models with headboard adjustable as individual backrests, are available from KELLER.

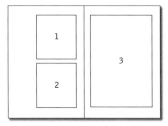

1. The Oblò model from the Italian
   company GALLI, in walnut. The
   designer is Enzo Berti.

2. Vela 2 Aluminium is a model
   from KD INTERIEUR. The wood
   is American cherry.

3. LUNA present versions of the Angelo model (above) and Luna model (below) without headboard.

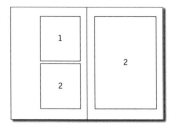

1. Another creation from GALLI, the Afro model in cherry wood.

2. Three models from the LUNA company. On this page: Premio. Overleaf: Maxx (top) and Pinin (below).

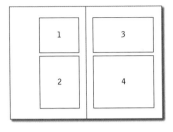

1. A model available from LUNA .

2. KELLER present this solid-frame bed without headboard.

3. The Corpus Ponte model is a product of the RUHE RAUM company.

4. Angelo is from the LUNA catalogue.

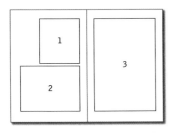

1. EMMEBI present this design by Sung Sook Kim: Ben, available with headboard fabric in several colours.

2. LEMA offer the Thur model.

3. The Petit model (above) and Jap (below) from LUNA.

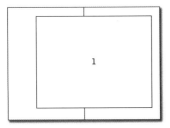

1. AZCUE present these models created by Abad Diseño.

MARIO BELLINI

Mario Bellini was born in 1935. A trained architect, he started to work as a designer in 1963. During his professional development, he has worked in these two areas simultaneously or has given priority to one or the other depending on the moment. As of the 1980's, he began to stand out more for his architecture. He has designed for different sectors such as for the automobile (Lancia and Fiat) or for illumination and furniture for brands such as Cassina, Artemide, B&B Italia, Yamaha, Rosenthal and Vitra among others.

Bellini has received numerous international prizes among which seven Golden Compass Awards stand out. Many of his works can be seen in the permanent collection of the Museum of Modern Art of New York which, in addition, dedicated a monographic exhibition to him in June 1987.

Profile

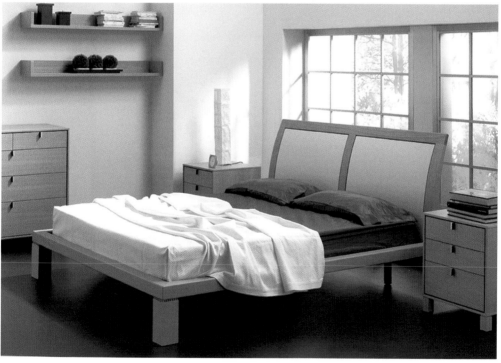

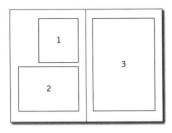

1. The Oltremare bed and Penisola bedside tables from PRESOTTO.

2. Nikka is from GRUPPO TISET-TANTA

3. The Yasmin model (above) and Wing model (below) from LUNA.

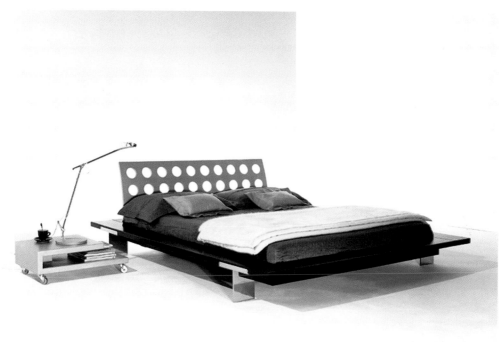

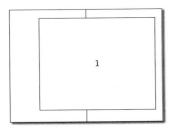

1. A model from PRESOTTO for
   minimalist settings.

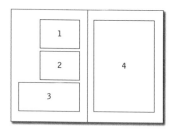

1. VERARDO offer this combination of Tosca and Essence.

2. Karma is a model in BONALDO's product range, created by Stefano Cavazzana.

3. Look and Diva, two models for the sleeping area from VERARDO.

4. The PRESOTTO catalogue includes these two bedroom models.

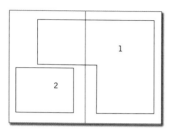

1. Paola Navone has designed Ebridil Arcipelago (left), Ebridi mattress (right) and Ebridi with headboard (below) for the ORIZ-ZONTI company.

2. VERARDO offer this combination for the bedroom: Shine+Deimos.

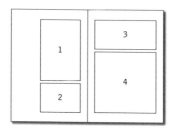

1. The Orbit model (above) and Raratong in white (below) from the house of KLENK.

2. Detail of Ele from INTERI, designed by Gabriel Teixidó.

3. Available from BELLATO is this creation by Luciano Bertoncini: Rem. Purity, rationality and diversity of size are the keynotes of this project consisting of beds and bedside tables. Rem comes entirely in anodized aluminium with the ring adjustable to two heights, 6.5 and 10.5 cm to hold the mattress in two different ways. The headboard is available in wengue, in light oak, in Macassar ebony or in aluminium grey or white lacquer.

4. Mustique is another design by Paola Navone for ORIZZONTI.

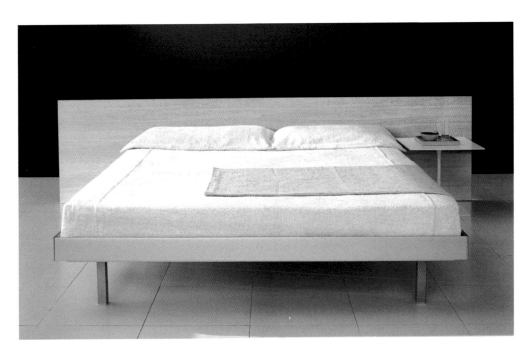

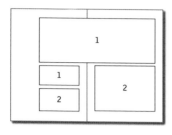

1. E15 bring us these models, created by Philipp Mainzer. Opposite, Karl, without headboard (top) in walnut, Lita (bottom), in European walnut. Overleaf, Mo, in oak.

2. Also from E15, a design by Philippe Allaeys: Noah, structure in European oak.

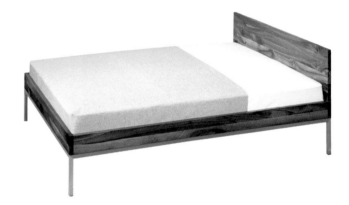

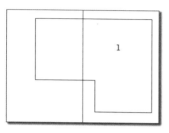

1. ORIZZONTI present these two models, created by Paola Navone. On this page (top) Cicladi Tatami. Bottom and overleaf, Adaman Tatami (top) and Adaman in wengue (bottom).

PAOLO PIVA

Paolo Piva is one of the most outstanding designers and architects on the international panorama who conceives his work as "a continual process initiated in consciousness". For Piva, a creation is, rather than merely the production of an idea, the development of permanent questioning of the theory of design. He was born in Adria in 1959 and studied architecture with Carlo Scarpa as his teacher in Venice. In this city and in Vienna, where he has set up studios, the two principal foci of Paolo Piva's professional activity are concentrated. He also teaches in the Academy of Applied Arts of Vienna. These two places also represent his main sources of inspiration and success. Apart from his work as an architect, Piva has created for some of the leading firms in the furnishing sector.

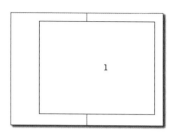

1. PORRO offer these two models
by Piero Lissoni. Standard, overleaf, top. The other illustrations
show different details of the Aero
model.

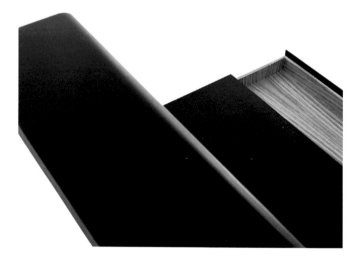

MATTEO THUN

Matteo Thun was born in 1952 in Bozen (South Tirol) and studied under the supervision of Oskar Kokoshka at the Salzburg Academia. He graduated in Architecture at the University of Florence in 1976 and some years later, in 1980, he
founded the Memphis Design Group along with Ettore Sottsass. From 1983 to
1996, he taught at the University of Applied Arts of Vienna while also working in
his own studio which he established in 1984 and which, today, has developed into a team of
50 architects, designers and graphic designers that undertake projects around the world.
Matteo Thun has always tried, in all of the areas in which he has developed his professional activity, to find more than a language in which to expound himself. His objective is to obtain
"echo and non-ego", which is to say transcendence rather than personal satisfaction.

Profile

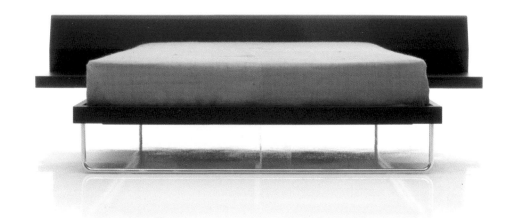

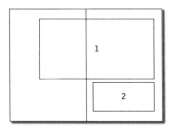

1. The Aero model from the PORRO company (right) and a detail of the headboard (left).

2. Burtscher & Bertolini are the creators of Sottiletto, from the HORM product range.

EMAF PROGETTI

Aurelio Zanotta set up Emaf in 1982. Since 1991, his successors have continued with his activity. The studio is mainly concerned with activities related to design, interior design, furniture, installations, image and product development, graphic art and communication for companies in the Real Estate sector. Their creations have been recognized at an international level and have been awarded numerous prizes and are also currently on view in the collections of a diversity of museums.

Profile

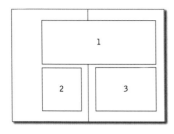

1. Opposite, the Eco bed designed by Emilio Nanni, which can be dismantled. From the same designer (right) the Zen model. Both are from ZANOTTA.

2. MOLTENI&C bring us this design by Paola Navone, belonging to a series of double beds available with four equally sized friezes, with or without headboard in a range of materials.

3. From GERVASONI's Inout collection, created and managed by Paola Navone.

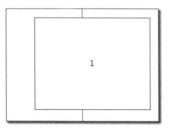

1. Eco is an anti-magnetic bed that can be taken apart, shown here with air-permeable mattress. Emilio Nanni created this model for ZANOTTA.

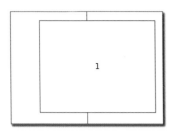

1. On these two pages, spring mattress and headboard from
   HORM, in minimalist style, design
   by Burtscher & Bertolini. Sottiletto is available in beech, in the
   picture shown with mocha stain.

   On the two following pages, vari-
   ous designs by Paola Navone for
   ORIZZONTI: (top left) Shima
   Cinque, and Shima Sette (top
   right). Also shown are Shima
   Quattro (bottom left) and Shima
   Sei (bottom right).

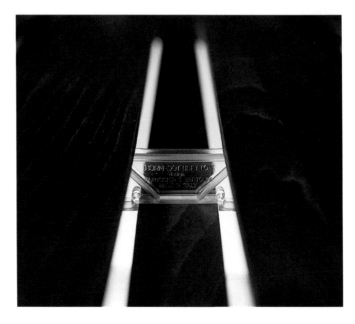

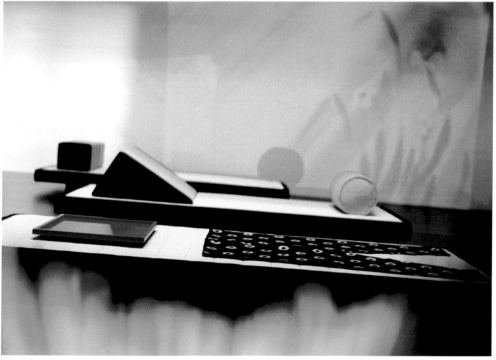

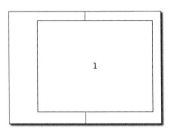

1. Different versions of the Legno-
letto model from ALIAS.

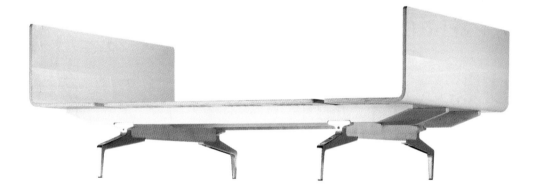

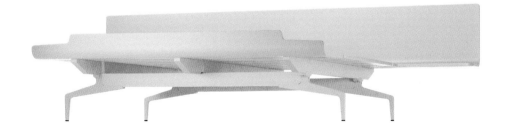

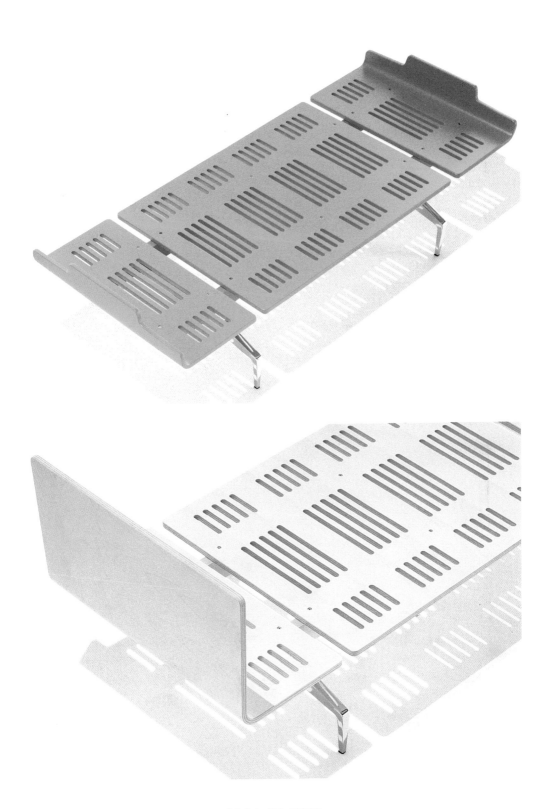

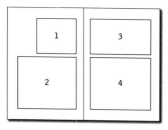

1. A design for children's bedroom from THE WHITE COMPANY.

2. Salina from the FLOU product range, designed by Rodolfo Dordoni.

3. Two beds, from ORIZZONTI. One can be extended.

4. ZANOTTA present this design by Emaf Progetti. The mattress comprises curved laminated beech, unstained, with rigidity adjusters inserted in nylon joints. The bed has a containing base which opens up, mechanically raising the mattress.

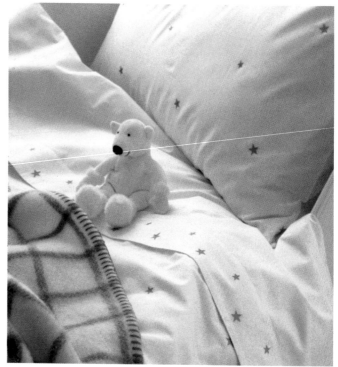

metal

Metal, traditionally, has been one of the materials most used to make beds. To the contrary of the case of other more modern or contemporary raw materials, it is less conditioning on the style. It is used to produce beds that range from the most classical of models to those of the most futuristic or industrial in appearance. In this section, we will find the latest designs from some of the top brands on the market that present a wide range of products as the fruit of the collaboration among the top designers on the international panorama and the top firms of the sector. Some proposals have been inspired in the forms of elegant old bedheads made in curved steel bars, whether silvery in color or lacquered, which give a more rustic air, but that undertake an exercise in the reinterpretation of designs of the past to become contemporary pieces that are suitable for the homes of today. Canopies have also been recovered. However, they are no longer an ornamental or overloaded element, but one that is reduced to a minimum expression and that has been given great expressiveness and creates a play with fabrics and net curtains. There are also those that have been conceived for minimalist atmospheres in which a simple structure frames the upper part of the piece as if it were a blank canvas. Zen philosophy, which is currently very popular, is also present on the following pages with futons on the floor that reduce this piece of furniture to its minimum expression. And we will see other beds which have not only been conceived to sleep in, but with their foldable backrests and sliding tables that allow you to work with the computer or breakfast in comfort as well.

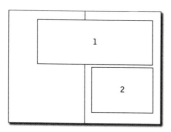

1. The PEROBELL company offers us this design by Lluís Codina: Global System.

2. A bed from ZANOTTA with an aluminium frame or a white-painted steel frame which can be dismantled. Also available in leather finish. Mini is from the studio of Emaf Progetti.

EILEEN GRAY

Eileen Gray (1878-1976) is considered to have been one of the most outstanding figures of the Modern Movement in France. She became involved in the world of design as a result of the studies she carried out in lacquering. She introduced the great dominion she acquired in this technique into artistic circles in Paris. She worked with some of the most relevant figures of the Modern Movement such as Le Corbusier and JJP Oud. She was also a pioneer in the use of chrome, steel tubes and glass in furniture. She exhibited her first designs in the same year as Mies van der Rohe and Marcel Breuer, and before Le Corbusier. In 1972, she was nominated Royal Designer to Industry by the Royal Society of Art in London. Her adjustable table "E1027" forms part of the collection of the Museum of Modern Art of New York.

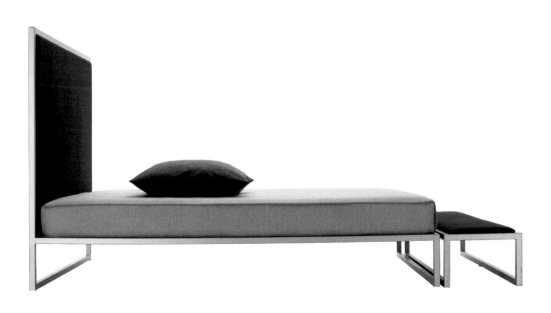

1. ALIAS present Decimo, created
   by Giandomenico Belotti.

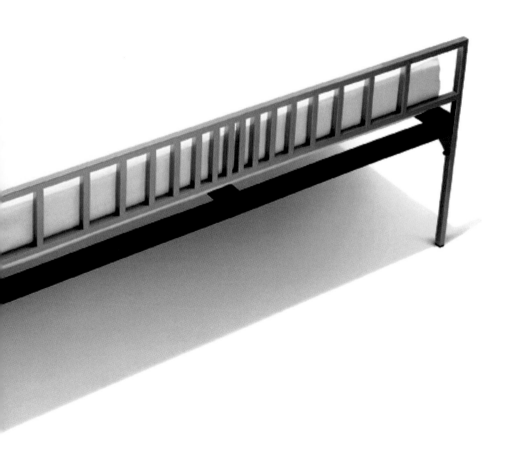

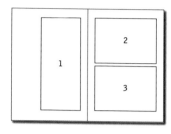

1. Detail of Nippon (above), a steel bed from PHILIPP PLEIN. Below, detail of the Kelly model, from the same company.

2. Lluís Codina has devised a bedroom furniture series based on versatile multipurpose components. Global System is a PEROBELL product.

3. Another version of the Mini model from ZANOTTA.

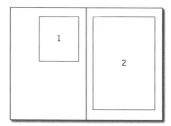

1. PHILIPP PLEIN features the Nippon model in their catalogue.

2. Summer Dream Bed (above) and Pasha are other models from PHILIPP PLEIN.

EMILIO NANNI

Emilio Nanni was born in Bazzano (Italy) in 1955. Within his professional career, he has worked in different areas such as architecture, design and painting. He graduated as an architect at the University of Florence in 1983 where he was to give classes from 1990 to 1998.

In 1984, he started his activity as designer of interiors, museums and fairs and undertook various private architectural interventions in different Italian cities. He has collaborated with companies such as Academia, Atelier, Bros's, Guzzini, MDF Italia, Montina, Progetti or Tonelli. He also works as image assessor and art director for various companies. As a painter, his works are exhibited as much in public as in private collections in a number of different countries.

Profile

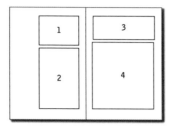

1. FLOU present Atlante.

2. CANTORI bring us these beds in a range of styles. The Gio (above).

3. A bed from the LUNA product range.

4. Sirius 2 (above) and Antlia (below), from the KD INTERIEUR collection.

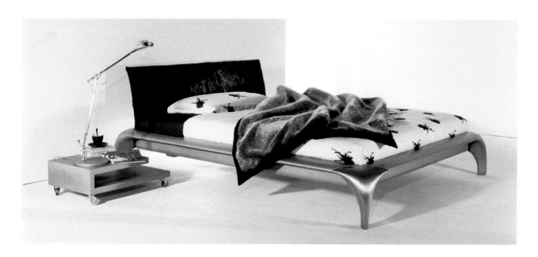

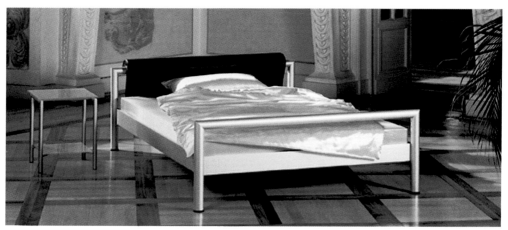

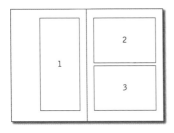

1. Opposite, various models from CANTORI. Above, Pascià, a classical design. The two pictures below show the Helios model.

2. ONE - WUSTLICH-DESIGN AG present this futuristic model.

3. Next, a model from the AUPING company, is by designer Ruud-Jan Kokke.

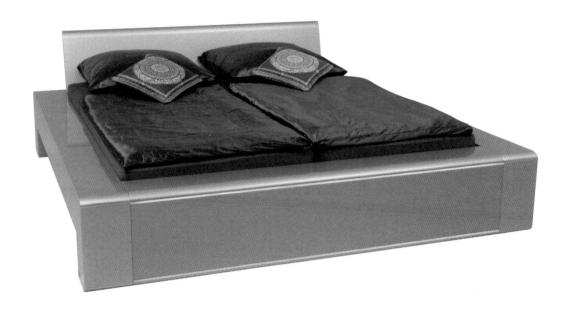

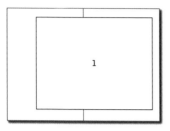

1. HORM bring us Capitano with a
   multipurpose collapsible bedside
   table.

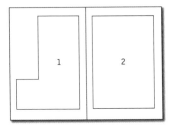

1. The bedside table of the Capitano model from HORM, which can be fitted on to the foot or the head of the bed.

2. Some models from the KD INTERIEUR product range: Quadrat 2 (above), Sirius 2 (centre), and another version of Quadrat (below).

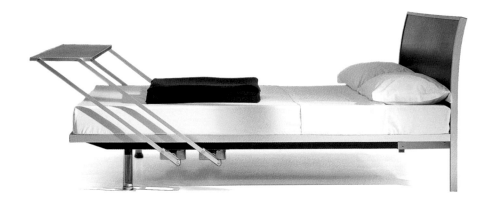

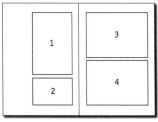

1. Daniel Thut designed this original folding and easily transportable model in the THUT range. Sheren Bett has a built-in light.

2. Casus is from the KD INTERIEUR catalogue.

3. Another design from THUT.

4. A bed designed in 1964 by A. G. Fronzoni. This model, from CAPPELLINI, bears the name of its designer.

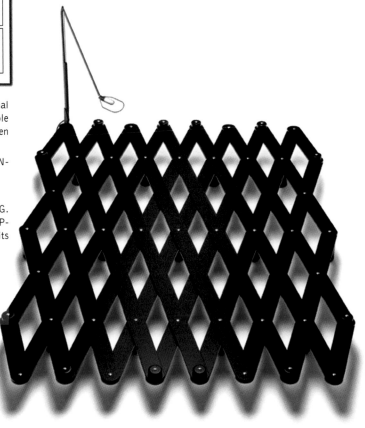

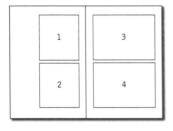

1. A canopy bed with a varnished white tubular frame. Orthopaedic base in poly laminated varnished beech. Two fabric-covered panels are inserted into the bed head to retain the pillows. Tule mosquito net with lower and upper sections in white cotton. Asseman is from DE PADOVA, created by Patrizia Cagliani.

2. This model is from ARCHDE-SIGN.

3. Skate System from ZALF.

4. The Bed 908 model from THUT.

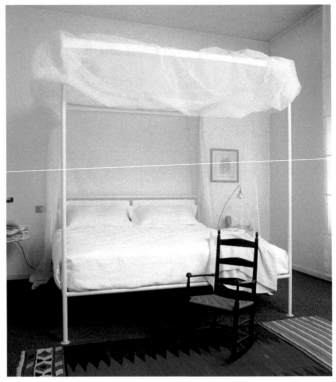

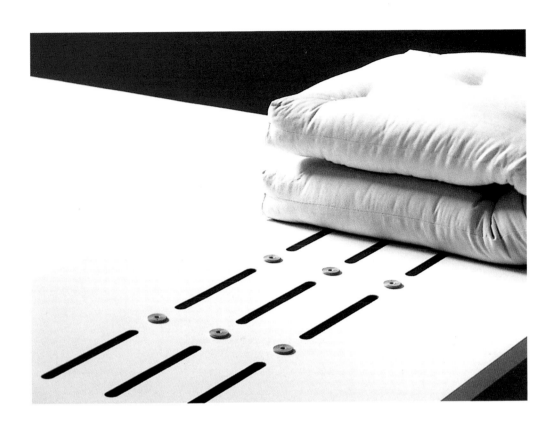

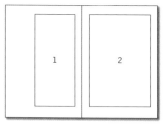

1. LATTOFLEX offers a wide range of products that adapt to the varying needs of the consumer. In these pictures: the Winx 300 model, allowing the feet or trunk to be elevated, or the adopting of a relaxing position between waking and sleeping, among others.

2. Orsi is another product of the ALIAS company, created by Giandomenico Belotti.

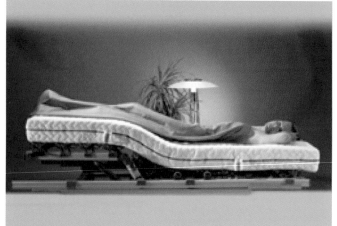

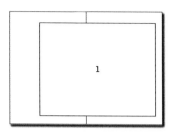

1. Different models from ARCHDE-
SIGN for the bedroom.

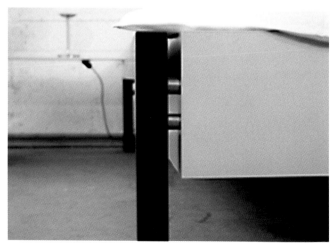

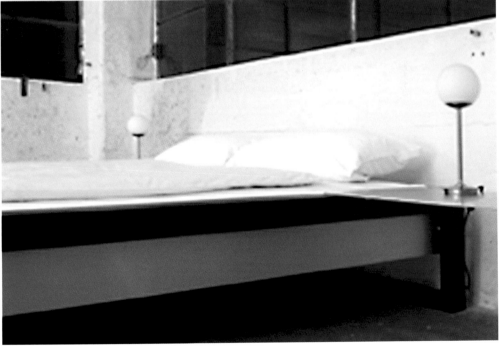

fabrics

In medieval times, tapestries and rich cloths were used in the bedheads and canopies that belonged to the more favored sectors of the population. In those times, this piece of furniture was considered a status symbol that was not available to all. Later, the materials were to go through different stages in which they lost or gained presence according to fashion and their designs have been adapted to stay in line with prevailing trends. Nowadays, fabrics have recovered ground from other traditional materials and there are a large number of models completely or partially covered in cloth. It has been the new technologies and investigation in the textile sector that has led to the broadening of the use of upholsteries which are much more resistant and in new original textures that generally make the beds more informal, colorful, versatile and warmer in appearance. The bedheads that we will see can basically be divided into two types: those that are padded and those which are not. In the first case, the bedhead becomes a backrest as comfortable as if it were a sofa and, in the second, more an element that adds beauty. A bed occupies a considerable amount of space that many have refused to waste for some time. We will also see some models that are also sofas or that have drawers below the mattress, which are becoming more practical and easier to use, and which provide storage space for either the bedclothes or for other objects.

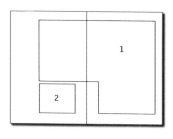

1. Patricia Urquiola has designed the Clip model (both pages, top) and Marais (bottom) for MOLTENI&C. The headboard of the Clip model can be lowered, and the bedside table can be adjusted to the structure of the bed as needed. Marais belongs to a series of single and double soft-filled beds with an original pyramid profile. Available also in fabric, velvet or leather.

2. IPE CAVALLI are the manufacturers of this model, created by designer R.Lazzeroni.

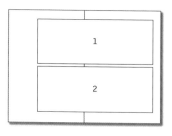

1. Caveau is brought to us by ZAN-OTTA. The exterior upholstery (cover) can be removed, and is available also in leather. In the 1852 and 1853 models the bed has a containing base which opens, raising the mattress mechanically.

2. A model from PRO SEDA.

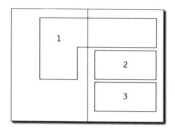

1. Jeffrey Bernett has created Metropolitan for B&B ITALIA; it comes in various colours.

2. Also from B&B ITALIA, a design by Paolo Piva, the Aletto model.

3. Breakfast, designed by Mario Bellini, is also from the B&B ITALIA catalogue.

KAZUHIDE TAKAHAMA

The name Kazuhide Takahama has been unseparable from Dino Gavina since the beginning of his career as a designer. Ever since they met in the Japanese fair for the Trienal de Milán in which they were introduced for the first time, a form of instantaneous understanding between the two has become established in spite of the lack of a common language. With the passing of the years, Takahama decided to move to Europe to work with Gavina and they became two of the major promoters of Italian design of the 1960's. He was to live in Bolonia of more than 30 years. His personality and his profession reflect and symbolize the meeting of two cultures: the oriental, in which he was educated, and the occidental, in which he had immersed himself. He created various companies for which he designed such as Gavina (1969), Simon International (1968) or Ultramobile (1996) among others.

Profile

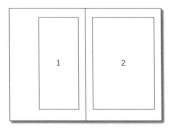

1. LIGNE ROSET present this design from Pascal Mourgue, Lover.

2. Flipper is a singular model from EMMEBI which can be put to different uses, thanks to the backrests situated at opposite corners.

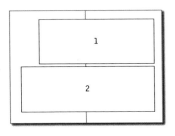

1. A model from the IVANO REDAELLI range. The upholstered base makes this a versatile item.

2. CASADESÚS CYCSA bring us the Laturka model, without legs (left) and Alma (right).

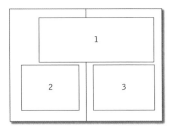

1. Emilio Nanni has created Zen for ZANOTTA. Special care has been taken with the bed's structure and the materials used to meet the parameters set by bio-architecture, eliminating metal. The paint used, too, is water-based.

2. POLIFORM bring us Moby, designed by Studio Kairos.

3. Marais: This creation by Paola Navone is available from MOLTENI & C.

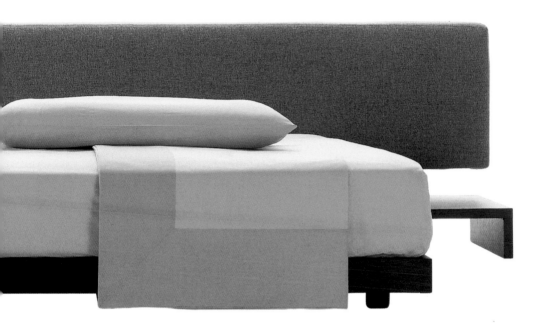

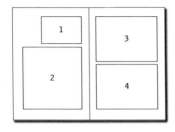

1. BONALDO produce the River model by Lino Codato.

2. Supersassi was designed by Matteo Thun for ROSSI DI ALBIZZATE.

3. The Charles model was designed by Antonio Citterio. Available from B&B ITALIA.

4. Jasper Morrison designed Sleeper, in the CAPPELLINI product range.

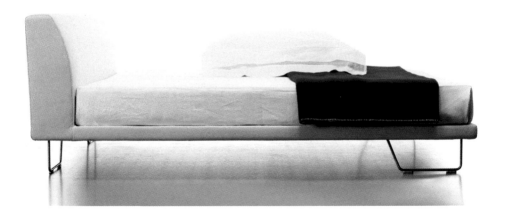

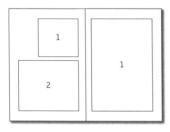

1. BONALDO offer us the models Cool (left) and Chillin (right), both designed by Stefano Cavazzana, Top. In the centre another model with green covers and, bottom, Fusion.

2. The Enea model for the EMME-BI label.

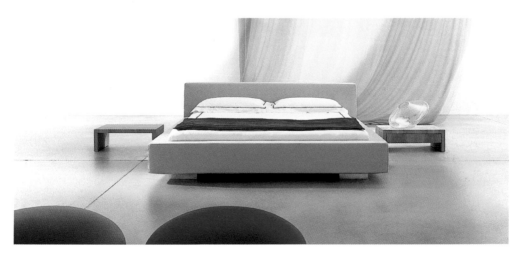

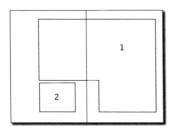

1. Different versions of the Somnus model by Paolo Piva, available from WITTMANN.

2. MOLTENI & C present Jean.

AFRA Y TOBIA SCARPA

Afra Bianchin (1937) and Tobia Scarpa (1935) have formed a team that has been a point of reference for the entire design world since 1958 when they started working in the glass sector for Venini in Murano. From among the pieces of furniture designed exclusively for Cassina, the armchair Soriano, which won the Golden Compass Award in 1970 and the armchair 925, which forms part of the permanent exhibition of the Museum of Modern Art in New York, stand out. They have also formed part of the Castiglioni team and designed for Flos. Of the pieces that they have produced for B&B Italia, Coronado and Erasmo are the best known. In addition to having also designed for Maxalto and Molteni, they have taken on responsibilities for the image campaigns of Benetton in Europe and America.

Profile

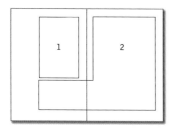

1. Deimos (above) and Deimos & Elliss (below) are from the VER- ARDO product range.

2. FLOU bring us these three mo- dels. On this page, a model for the bedroom, designed by Rodolfo Dordoni. On the right, another creation by this Italian designer, Bold. Top, Sailor by Carlo Colom- bo.

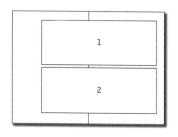

1. Eliot is produced by MÖLLER DESIGN, designed by Cord Möller-Ewerbeck. Available in a range of colours.

2. GIORGETTI bring us this creation by Antonello Mosca: Hermitage.

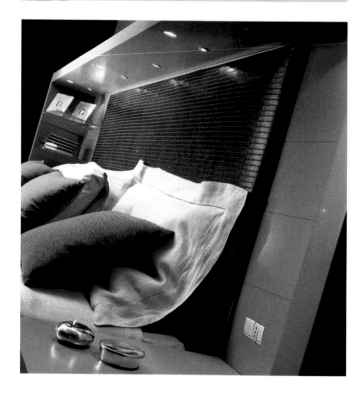

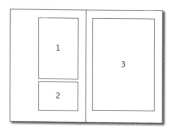

1. A model from MOON FIRE-WORK, in white and red.

2. Rodolfo Dordoni created the FAVIGNANA model available from the FLOU.

3. One of the latest models in the REDAELLI range. Noted for its versatility.

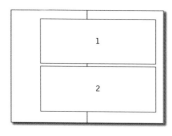

1. A model from the AUPING range, one of the most innovative on the market. The company produces computarised beds, with airconditioning and different positions that can be remote control operated, among other options.

2. The FRAUFLEX company brings us this model.

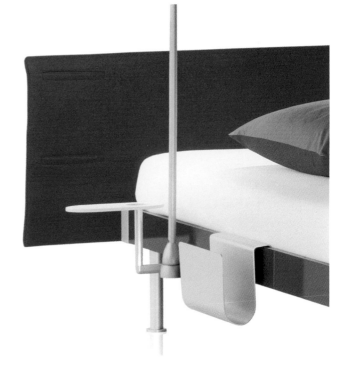

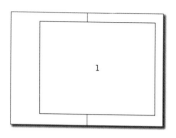

1. Segno was designed by Carlo
   Colombo for CAPPELLINI. This
   model forms a part of a collection of beds of different sizes
   with, wooden, metal and
   polyurothene structure.

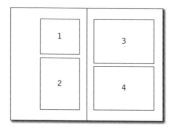

1. Ebridi High, a design by Paola Navone, is a model from the ORIZZONTI product range.

2. Two models from PRESOTTO. Above, a combination of the Reflex bed and the Kubo bedside tables.

3. Blue is a bed from the LUNA catalogue.

Perseus 2 is available from KD INTERIEU. It comes in different finishes; shown here with aluminium and velvet.

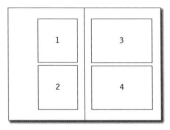

1. Shetland is a creation by designer Paola Navone for ORIZZONTI.

2. Another version of Segno by Carlo Colombo, available from CAPPELLINI.

3. DEMA bring us this bed from the Hotelo collection.

4. Lo Scalzo Moscheri designed Net for GALLI, a model that has removable covers.

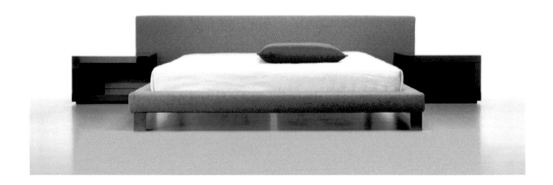

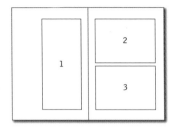

1. Two designs from RUHE RAUM.
2. DOIMO INTERNATIONAL produce this model.
3. ORIZZONTI presen this design by Gigi&Chiara and Tanzi: Maddalen Due.

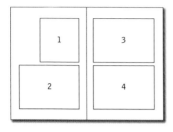

1. Samoa is from the ORIZZONTI catalogue. It's a creation by Giulio Manzoni.

2. A model designed by Rodolfo Dordoni, and available from FLOU.

3. GRUPPO TISETTANTA present the Japo model.

4. Archilab is the creator of Lythe, a model from the IPE CAVALLI product range.

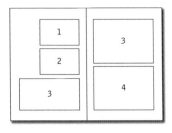

1. The VITTORIO BONACINA company and their Flo model.

2. Carlo Colombo is the creator of Grande, a bed in the CAPPELLI-NI product range with a wood and metal structure with a loose cover available in different materials.

3. ZANOTTA bring us Invisible, a creation by I-Bride (2002), available with or without headboard, both this unit and the structure of the bed are covered in pure merino wool.

4. Impero was designed by Emaf Progetti for ZANOTTA. The fabric is polyurethane/ Du Pont Dacron.

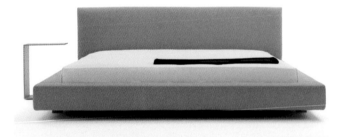

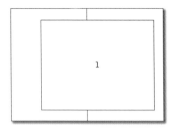

1. Alfa Letto is a bed from the ZANOTTA product range, created by Emaf Progetti. The height can be varied by adjusting the feet. The pouf is convertible into an extension of the headboard or bedside table.

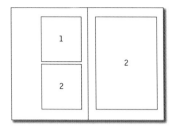

1. Detail of the Zen headboard in polyurethane/Du Pont Dacron.

and the shelf which is at the same level as the structure of the bed. ZANOTTA produce this model by Emilio Nanni which is anti-magnetic.

2. VITTORIO BONACINA bring us these models. Overleaf, top, a design by P. Azzolini and P. Tinuper: Theta. Bottom, Basic Theta Young.

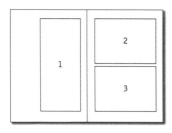

1. GRUPPO TISETTANTA present some of their complements for the Halifax label, in the Them collection.

2. A composition consisting of different elements in the Puzzle System from MIXEL in the GRUPPO TISETTANTA . For children's bedrooms.

3. Composition from the City Line system from DOIMO INTERNATIONAL. Th bed is upholstered in lilac cream.

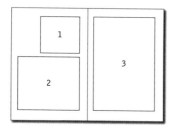

1. A composition from ZALF for young people, from the Domino programme.

2. Duetto are two beds in one, from the FLOU company, occupying the minimum of space.

3. Another design from ZALF's young people's collection, Altera (above). Below, a combination of Link and Skate System.

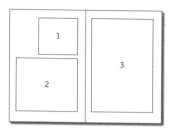

1. Panarea is a product from the ORIZZONTI catalogue

2. A child's bed from BONALDO. With slip cover and pockets for computers, designed by Cr&s Bonaldo: the Pongo model.

3. Paola Navone is the creator of Smilan Tessile (top), a single bed with simple lines, available from ORIZZONTI, and Milos, with padded headboard.

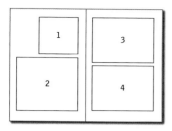

1. FRAUFLEX produce this model with its sinuous lines, designed by Sandi Renko: Frau-Kathrin.

2. ZALF includes Monopoli in its product range.

3. Désirée is a bed from WK WOHNEN, designed by Anette Lang.

4. Oltremare and Kalipso drawers from PRESOTTO.

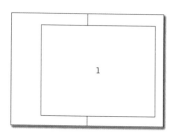

1. Different models from the German company BRETZ, the second most well-known brand of this nationality in the sector. Bretz Brothers Design has created these models, as they put it, "for wild hearts". Adjacent, from top to bottom: Gaudi, Lucky Paisley and Gaudi Sonnen. Overleaf, Mammut (top) and Mammut Rose (bottom).

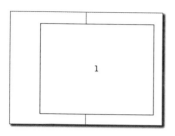

1. More models from the BRETZ label. This page, top, Alibaba Rose. In the centre, Monster and, below, Lucky Flowers. Overleaf, Monster Zebra (top) and Alibaba Arcan (bottom).

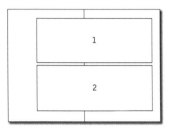

1. A model from the FRAUFLEX
   company. On the left, a detail of
   the headboard with removable
   pillows, converting it into a soft
   backrest.

2. Luciano Bertoncini designed Rem
   for BELLATO, included in that
   company's High Tech collection.

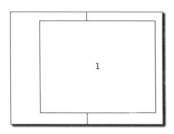

1. Capreara (two illustrations, top) is manufactured by ORIZZONTI'. Bottom left, also from this Italian firm is Bahamas Alto and, bottom right, Bahamas Basso.

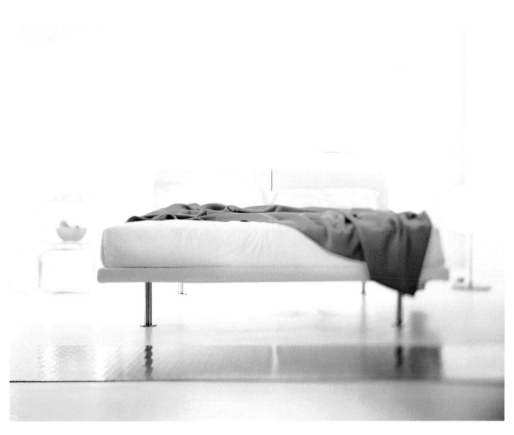

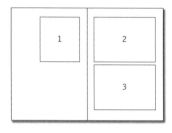

1. Sober, a model designed by Héctor Diego: timeless, geometric.

2. Carlo Colombo is the creator of Sailor, available from FLOU.

3. DE PADOVA produce this design by Vico Magistretti, Pilgrim. The headboard consists of a metal structure covered with polyurethane foam. It has a base which can be taken apart with polyester lining. The mattress is tubular steel with laminated beech. This model is easy to move thanks to two castors that can be locked into position. The headboard cover can be completely removed.

STEFAN HEILIGER

Was born in 1941 in Berlin. He worked for Mercedes Benz from 1964 to 1977. During this time, he also maintained a teaching activity. In 1978, he set up his own design studio and intensified his activity as a furniture designer. He has worked for a number of prestigious companies in the sector such as Bonaldo, Rolf Benz, Leolux or Interprofil. He has been awarded with numerous prizes. His works reveal a special interest for innovation in functional sofas: convertible, such as sofa beds, armchairs for relax and divans. Since the year 2000, he has started his own furniture collection that is characterized by the simple lightweight pieces that it contains.

Profile

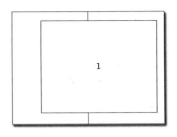

1. Three models from FLOU. Above, Nathalie by Italian designer Vico Magistretti, which is eminently easy to store. Below, two designs from Rodolfo Dordoni, on the left, Marettimo and, on the right, Orchidea.

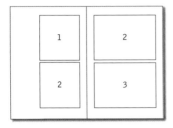

1. Taj is from the BONALDO catalogue and was designed by Stefano Cavazzana.

2. A creation by Vico Magistretti for
   FLOU. Overleaf, top, the Nathalie
   model in white, from the same
   manufacturer and designer.

3. Levanzo, by Rodolfo Dordoni for
   FLOU.

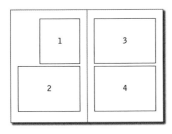

1. Palatino is available at VINÇON stores, from FLORA FRANCH BESOLI.

2. At VINÇON you can also find this bed courtesy of CONFORTEC.

3. Designer Mario Bellini created this model, Breakfast, for B&B ITALIA.

4. A composition for young people from ZALF, part of the GRUPPO EUROMOBIL.

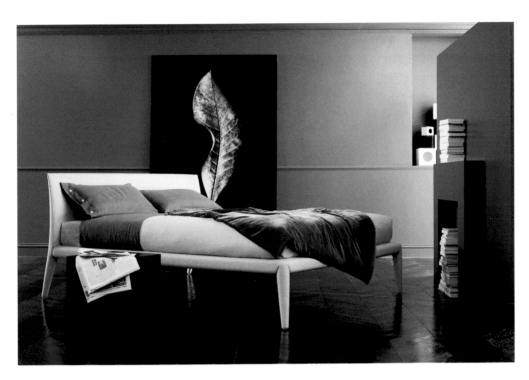

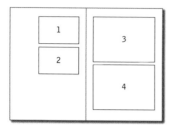

1. Antonio Citterio designed the Charles model for B&B ITALIA.

2. Relaxin is a bed from the house of BONALDO.

3. Teo is another creation by designer Paolo Piva, in this case produced by POLIFORM. This model is available in different types of wood (American cherry, wengue and oak).

4. Another model from POLIFORM for bedroom areas.

ANTONELLO MOSCA

Born and trained in architecture in Milan, Antonello Mosca started to concentrate on interior design in 1964. After having formed part of the editorial staff of various publications within the sector such as Casabella and Domus, in 1969, he created Casamica -- the first publication dedicated to Italian furniture with a sizable circulation. He currently collaborates with a diversity of newspapers and magazines and directs a television program. He has received awards for his activities in the media on various occasions. As an industrial designer, he has collaborated with Cinova, Giorgetti, Tisettanta, Flou, Ycami Collection, and Minotti among others. His activity has extended to the design of showrooms and to consultant to large stores. In the textile sector, after a long experience with Bayer, he collaborates with different prestigious companies under the name of Tessilforum.

Profile

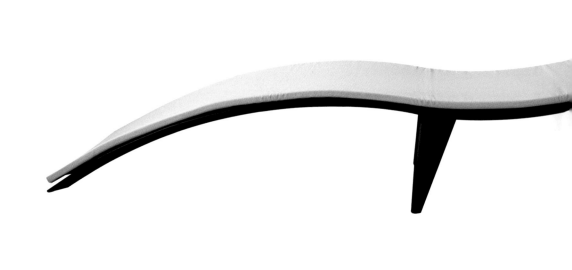

day bed

Divans are among the most suggestive pieces of furniture. The French have spread their chaise longue all over the world and, with this term, they have made its aspect of chair with an elongated seat stand out. In English, on the other hand, it is referred to as a day bed. In Spanish, it is called diván, from the Arabic díwán, and has been associated, since the birth of Psychoanalysis, with psychological therapy. Freud started to use it with his patients as it allowed them to lie down completely and relax in a posture that they identified with sleep. In this way, he found that they were more able to connect with their most intimate inner self. It has never been a piece of furniture of popular use. On the contrary, it has generally been used by those with more resources and who, maybe for this reason, have had more time for contemplation, reading and resting. However, over the last few decades, its design has evolved tremendously. A lot of imagination has led to a range of models full of originality. There are models ranging from the most informal to the most sophisticated, those that recover classical forms, those with oriental influences... They are, whatever the case may be, pieces that have been conceived for a diversity of uses among which we find the highly recommended Mediterranean siesta.

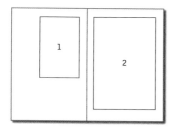

1. Designer Ramón Esteve created
   Cuadrado in the Babia Collection
   for GANDIA BLASCO.

2. The models Teki (top) and Space +
   Book (bottom) from VERARDO.

PIERO LISSONI

Piero Lissoni was born in 1956. Having finalized his studies in Architecture at
the University of Milan, he started to work for Molteni and Lema. In 1986, he
established the Lissoni studio in Milan along with Nicoletta Canesi where he
developed projects in architecture, interior design, graphic design, industrial
design and art direction and corporate image for some of the most outstanding
companies of the sector. Some of the companies with which Lissoni has collaborated are Porro,
Living, Matteograssi, Bofia Cucine, Artemide, Foscarini, Kartell, Driade, Cassina or the
Benetton Group. Piero Lissoni is one of the most outstanding figures in the world of Italian
design inspired by minimalism. However, he would reject this label in an attempt to escape from
the limitations that it would imply and prefers to talk about simplicity. Concepts such as the
honesty and purity of form are also essential to his creations.

Profile

Only Beds 247 DAY BED

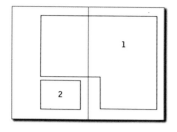

1. Lobby: an award-winning sofa that converts into a bed, from BRÜHL. The back and arm rests fold into the base, by exerting light pressure on them. Designed by Siegfried Bensinger.

2. Also from BRÜHL, Moule in red.

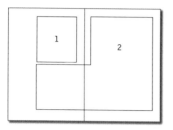

1. Il Refugio is a design from the hand of Luca Sacchetti, part of his collection Dreams.

2. BRF bring us this flexible model created by Tim Power, Flip, which converts into a single or double bed, as required.

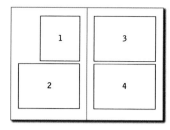

1. Modena is a folding model from PHILIPP PLEIN.

2. SEEFELDER produce this piece of furniture, notable for its versatility. The Layla model is a design by Laprell & Classen.

3. This model from SANTA & COLE was designed by Kazuhide Takahama. It has a solid wood structure with curved birch laths and a mattress with a removable cover.

4. Andaman Dormeuse by Paola Navone is from ORIZZONTI.

Only Beds 253 D A Y   B E D

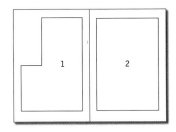

1. Tonga Divano (top) and Tonga Dormeuse (bottom) are from the ORIZZONTI catalogue and designed by Giulio Manzoni.

2. LIGNE ROSET bring us this oh so versatile creation by Arik Lev: Arik. This model is easy converted into a bed.

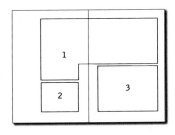

1. HORM present Line by Carlo Cumini, in black and white with a headrest.

2. Maniglia Onda is from GALLI.

3. A model from REDAELLI.

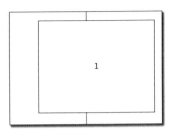

1. BRÜHL produce this model, Jeff, by Johannes Foersom & Peter Hiort-Lorenzen (adjacent). Below, Orit by Siegfried Bensinger. Overleaf, different versions of Jerry by Roland Meyer-Brühl.

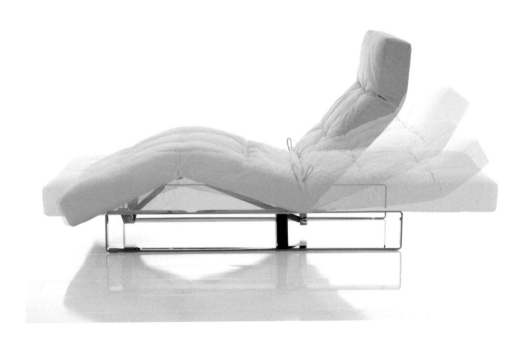

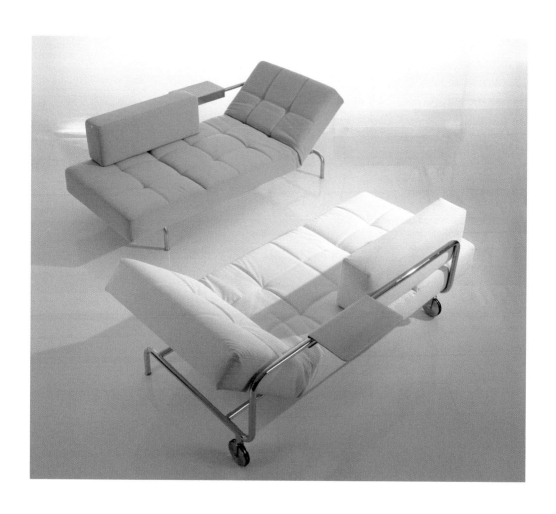

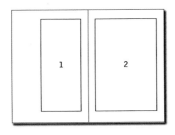

1. Day bed Obsession (above) and Day bed Lust (below) from PHILIPP PLEIN.

2. Jerry in pistachio green and Orit, two models from BRÜHL.

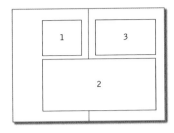

1. Day bed Lust from PHILIPP PLEIN, in black.

2. Another model from PHILIPP PLEIN: Obsession (left) and Lust, in a shade of brown (right).

3. DE PADOVA produce the Capitonné pouf. Its size (120 x 150 cm) make it suitable for a range of uses. The structure is wood, the filling is expanded polyurethene and covered in leather.

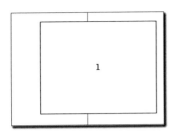

1. Different bed designs from BONALDO which are totally right for the living room: Centouno (top), Fata (centre) and Pisolo (below). Overleaf, Ragià (top) and Teddy, by Peter Ross, from the same company.

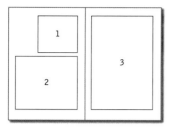

1. Another version of Moule from BRÜHL.

2. ORIZZONTI present this design by Paola Navone: White Hight.

3. Orit (top) and Jeff (below) are two models from BRÜHL.

1. Clai is from BRÜHL.

2. A model from AZCUE's Bitter Duplo Programme.

3. Day bed from one of CAPPELLI-NI.'s Sistema Notte range.

4. Mimic, created by Volker Laprell and Volker Classen for BRÜHL, in white and red, is easily converted into a bed, by exerting pressure on the armrests and backrest.

TODD BRACHER

Todd Bracher was born in New York and, after having spent some time in Denmarks Designskole (Denmark), he settled in Italy. He graduated with honors at the Pratt Institute of New York after four years of study. He has worked as a designer and for various consultancies in Italy, Denmark and New York. For his creations, he has received numerous international distinctions among which are the ID Award (2000) for Open Privacy; his chair Bloom has been a prize winner on four occasions: Promosedia Design for the European Chair Competition (Udine, Italy), Idee Award of 2001 (Tokyo, Japan), ID Award of 2002 (New York, USA) and the UNESCO Design 21 Award (Paris, France).

Profile

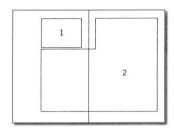

1. Croco 14 in the Inout Collection from GERVASONI.
2. Two canopy beds from the DE-DON Daydream Collection.

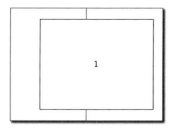

1. Croco 82 is produced by the Italian GERVASONI company.

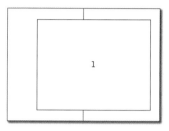

1. Freud is available from ZANOT-TA, created by Todd Bracher, upholstered in flameproof fabric. Also available in leather.

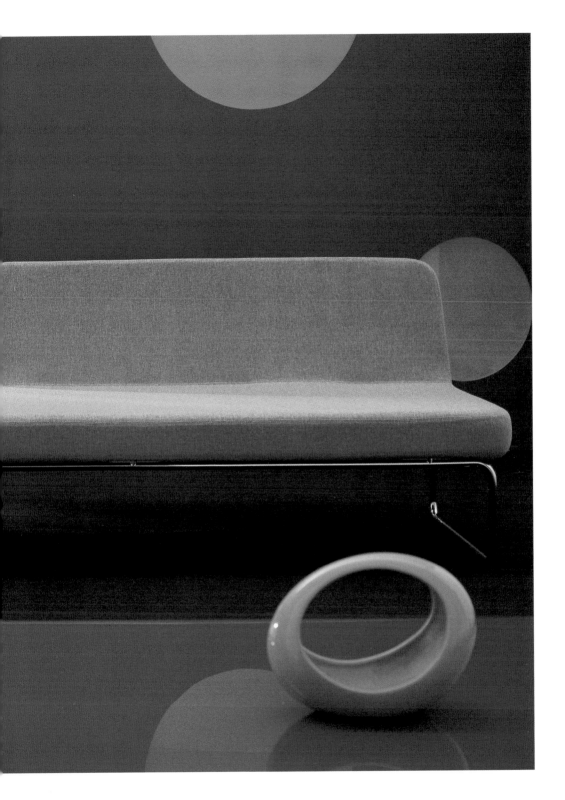

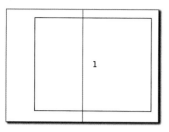

1. Luna chaise longue (this page).
Overleaf, Chill, from GANDIA
BLASCO.

FRANCESCO BINFARÉ

Francesco Binfaré was educated under his father's supervision. He started to work for Cassina in 1960. At first, he was investigator into new technologies and later, he became Cesare's assistant for new projects and made prototypes. In 1969, He was appointed director of the Cassina Center and helped in giving birth to some classic designs such as Up 5 by Gaetano Pesce (1969).

In 1980, he created the Center of Design and Communication to develop projects. He has participated in the most outstanding projects that have been undertaken by Cassina such as Wink by Toshiyuki Kita, Tramonto to New York, Feltri by Gaetano Pesce and Torso by Paolo Deganello. He later designed for Edra and Adele C.Painting.

Profile

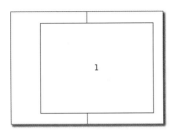

1. GANDIA BLASCO offers these original designs. Opposite, Paper Mountain, designed by J.M.Ferrero, with micropearl filling. On the right, the Na Xemena chaise longue. And, bottom, two nordic quilts created by J.A.Gandía.

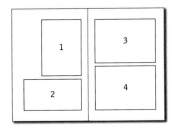

1. Isabelle Leijin has designed these two models.
2. Perfo is a day bed from RÖ, designed by Hans Eichenberger.
3. A divan from DEMA's Hotello collection, designed by C.Bimbi.
4. ZALF include these models in their catalogue.

   Overleaf and subsequent pages:

   Day bed from one of CAPPELLI-NI.'s Sistema Notte range.

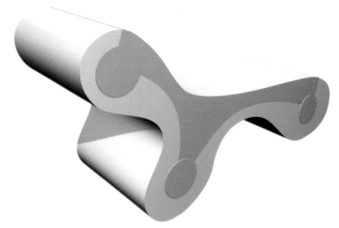

directory

ALIAS
Via dei Videtti 2
24064 Grumello del Monte (BG)
ITALY
Tel. 39 0 354 422 507
info@aliasdesign.it
www.aliasdesign.it

ARCAYA EQUIP (Distribute in
Spain: MOLTENI and MINOTTI.)
San Martín, 1 Bajo Trasera
01130 Álava
SPAIN
Tel. 34 945 462 408
Fax. 34 945 462 446
arcaya@jet.es

ARCHDESIGN (See P2 ARCHDE-
SIGN)

AUPING
Laan van Borgele, 70
7415 DK Deventer
THE NETHERLANDS
verkoop@auping.nl
www.auping.com

AZCUE
Apdo. de correos 520730
Azpeitia (Gipuzcoa)
SPAIN
Tel. 34 943 151 500
Fax. 34 943 816 204
info@azcue.com
www.azcue.com

B&B ITALIA
Strada provinciale 32, 15
22060 Novedrate (Co)
ITALY
Tel. 39 031 795 213
Fax. 39 031 795 224
beb@bebitalia.it
www.bebitalia.it

BELLATO (See PALLUCCO.)

BERNINI
Via Milano 8
20020 Ceriano Lagnetto (Mi)
ITALY
Tel. 39 296 469 293
Fax. 39 296 469 293
info@bernini.it
www.bernini.it

BIS BIS IMPORTS BOSTON
4 Park Plaza
MA 02116 Boston
U.S.A.
Tel. 1 6 173 507 565
Fax. 1 6 174 822 339
info@bisbis.com

BONALDO
Via Straelle 3
35010 Villanova (PD)
ITALY
Tel. 39 0 499 299 011
Fax. 39 0 499 299 000
bonaldo@bonaldo.it
www.bonaldo.it

BRETZ
Alexander-Bretz-Strasse 2
55457 Gensingen
GERMANY
Tel. 49 67 278 950
Fax. 49 67 271 030
cultsofa@bretz.de
www.bretz.de

BRF
Loc. S. Marziale
53034 Colle Val d'Elsa (SI)
ITALY
Tel. 39 0 577 929 418
Fax. 39 0 577 929 648
info@brfcolors.com
www.brfcolors.com

BRÜHL & SIPPOLD
95138 Bad Steben-Carlsgrün
GERMANY
Tel. 49 09 288/955-0
Fax. 49 09 288/95 599
bruehl@bruehlsippold.de
www.bruehlsippold.de

CANTORI
Via Dante Alighieri, 52
60021 Camerano (An)
ITALY
Tel. 39 071 730 051
Fax. 39 0 717 300 501
info@cantori.it
www.cantori.it

CAPPELLINI
Tel. 39 031 759 111

cappellini@cappellini.it
www.cappellini.it

CASADESÚS - CYCSA
Luxemburgo 19
08769 Castellví de Rosanes (Barcelona)
SPAIN
Tel. 34 937 735 660
info@cycsa.es
www.cycsa.es

CATTELAN ITALIA
Via Pilastri 15
36010 Carré (VI)
ITALY
Tel. 39 04 453 187 711
Fax. 39 0 445 314 289
info@cattelanitalia.com
www.cattelanitalia.com

CLUB8COMPANY
Fabriksvej 4
P.O. Box 74
6870 Ogold
DENMARK
Tel. 45 70 131 366
Fax. 45 7 013 136
club8@club8.com
www.club8.com

BoConcept® København
Gl. Kongevej 29ª
1610 København V
DENMARK
Tel. 45 3326 8787
Fax 45 3323 8787
copenhagen.city.dk@boconcept.com
En SPAIN: www.boconcept.com

DEDON
Zeppelinstraße 22
21337 Lüneburg
GERMANY
Tel. 49 04 131 699 690
office@dedon.de
www.dedon.de

DEDON ESPAÑA
Aragón 333
08009 Barcelona
SPAIN
Tel. 34 932 080 903
Fax. 34 934 583 197
spain@dedon.de

DEDON ESPAÑA
Aragón 333
08009 Barcelona
SPAIN
Tel. 34 932 080 903
Fax. 34 934 583 197
spain@dedon.de

DEMA
Via dellè Città, 33
50052 Certaldo (FI)
ITALY
Tel. 39 0 571/6 511 232
Fax. 39 0 571/651 233
info@dema.it
www.dema.it

DE PADOVA
Corso Venezia 14
20121 Milano
ITALY
Tel. 39 02 777 201
Fax. 39 0 277 720 280
clienti@depadova.it
www.depadova.it

DI LIDDO & PEREGO
Via Trieste 71
20036 Meda (MI)
ITALY
Tel. 39 0 362 342 290
Fax. 39 0 362 340 320
info@diliddoeperego.it
www.diliddoeperego.it

DOIMO INTERNATIONAL GROUP
Via Montegrappa, 90
31010 Mosnigo di Moriago (TV)
ITALY
Tel. 39 0 438 890 699
Fax. 39 0 438 890 121
doimointernational@doimo.it
www.gruppodoimo.com

E 15
Hospitalstrasse 4
61440 Oberursel
GERMANY
Tel. 49 0 617 197 950
Fax. 49 06 171 979 590
e15@e15.com
www.e15.com

ELITE
Viale Trento, 59/A

33077 Sacile (PN)
ITALY
Tel. 39 0 434 738 092
Fax. 39 0 434 781 057
info@elite-srl.it
www.elite-srl.it

EMMEBI
Via C. Monteverdi, 28
20031 Cesano Maderno (MI)
ITALY
Tel. 39 0 362 502 296
Fax. 39 0 362 509 602
info@emmebidesign.com
www.emmebidesign.com

FLOU
Via Luigi Cadorna 12
20036 Meda (Mi)
ITALY
Tel. 39 03 623 731
Fax. 39 0 362 343 199
infoflou@flou.it
www.flou.it

FORMER
Via per Cantù, 43
20060 Montesolaro di Carimate
(Como)
ITALY
former@former.it
www.former.it

FRAUFLEX
Via dell'Artigianato 35/36
46047 Bancole di Porto Mantovano
(MN)
ITALY
Tel. 39 0 376 399 399
Fax. 39 0 376 390 855
www.frauflex.it

GALLI
Via Volta 3
22060 Carugo
ITALY
Tel. 39 031 761 368
Fax. 39 031 762 258
info@gallimobili.it
www.gallimobili.it

GANDÍA BLASCO
Músico Vert, 4
46870 Ontinyent (Valencia)
SPAIN

Tel. 34 962 911 320
Fax. 34 962 913 044
gandiablasco@gandiablasco.com
www.gandiablasco.com

GERVASONI
Zona Industriale Udinese
33050 Pavia de Undinese
ITALY
Tel. 39 0 432 656 611
Fax. 39 0 432 656 612
info@gervasoni1882.com
www.gervasoni1882.com

GIORGETTI
Via Manzoni, 20
20036 Meda (MI)
ITALY
Tel. 39 036 275 275
Fax. 39 036 275 575
giorspa@giorgetti-spa.it
www.giorgetti-spa.it

HÉCTOR DIEGO (Design studio. His
designs are produced by PEROBELL,
GRANVIA, VICCARBE...)
C/ Alcoceber 1, pta 23 B
46011 Valencia
SPAIN
Tel. 34 963 268 200
Fax. 34 963 268 200
contact@hectordiego.com
www.hectordiego.com

HORM
Via San Giuseppe 25
33082 Azzano Decimo (Pordenone)
ITALY
horm@horm.it
www.horm.it

INGO MAURER
Kaiserstrasse 47
80801 München
GERMANY
Tel. 49 893 816 06 – 0
Fax: 49 893 81 606 20
info@ingo-maurer.com

INTERI
Ctra. De Villena, Km 2,5
Apdo. 119
30510 Yecla
SPAIN
Tel. 34 968 751 011
Fax. 34 968 751 588
mobilfresno@mobilfresno.com
www.interi.es

IPE CAVALLI
Via Mattei, 1
Via Roma 57
40069 Zola Predosa (Bologna)
ITALY
Tel. 39 051 753 845
Fax. 39 0 516 186 310
ipe@ipe.it
www.ipe-cavalli.com

ISABELLE LEIJN (Estudio de diseño)
Vrolikstraat 355c
1092TB Amsterdam
THE NETHERLANDS
Tel. 31 0 206 751 654
iLstudio@leijn.com
www.leijn.com

IVANO REDAELLI (Ver REDAE-
LLI.)

JUVENTA
Slipstraat, 4
8880 Ledegem
BELGIUM
Tel. 32 56 500 191
Fax. 32 56 503 937
juventa@juventa.be
www.juventa-designedforyou.com

KD INTERIEUR
Sandershäuserstr. 34
34123 Kassel
GERMANY
Tel. 49 056 153 992
Fax. 49 056 154 869
info@kd-interieur.de
www.kd-interieur.com

KELLER
Mühlweg 25/3
71711 Murr
GERMANY
Tel. 49 07 144 849 964

Fax. 49 07 144 849 966
info@keller-quality-concept.de

KLENK WHON KOLLECTIONEN
Industriestrasse 34
72221 Haiterbach
GERMANY
Tel. 49 745 693 820
Fax. 49 7 456 938 240
info@klenk-collection.de
www.klenk-collection.de

LAGO
Via Morosini, 22-24
35010 San Giorgio in Bosco (Padova)
ITALY
info@lago.it
www.lago.it

LATTOFLEX (Export: Thomas GmbH
+ Co. Sitz- und Liegemöbel KG)
Walkmühlenstraße 93
27432 Bremervörde
GERMANY
Tel. 49 4 761 979 138
Fax. 49 4 761 979 538
www.lattoflex.de

LEMA
Strada Statale Briantea
22040 Alzate Brianza
ITALY
Tel. 39 031 630 990
Fax. 39 031 632 492
lema@lemamobili.com
www.lemamobili.com

LIGNE ROSET (for address in Ger-
many, see ROSET MÖBEL)
B.P. N° 9
01470 Briod
FRANCE
Tel. 33 0 474 361 700
Fax. 33 0 474 361 695
www.ligne-roset.fr

LUCA SACCHETTI (Designer)
Via Bramante, 29
20154 Milano
ITALY
Tel. 39 023 496 141

LUNA
Hansaring 88
50670 Köln

GERMANY
Tel. 49 2 211 260 196
Fax. 49 2 211 260 198
www.luna-betten.de

MATTEOGRASSI
Via Padre Rovanati, 2
22066 Mariano Comense
ITALY
Tel. 39 031 757 711
Fax. 39 031 748 388
info@matteograssi.it
www.matteograssi.it

MINOTTI (See ARCAYA EQUIP,
agents in Spain.)
Via Indipendenza 152
P.O. Box Numero 61
20036 Meda (MI)
ITALY
Tel. 39 0 362 343 499
Fax. 39 0 362 340 319
info@minotti.it
www.minotti.com

MIXEL (TISETTANTA)
Via Tofane, 37
20034 Giussano (Milano)
ITALY
Tel. 39 03 623 191
Fax. 39 0 362 319 330
info@tisettanta.it

MOBILIFICIO PREALPI
Via Fossa 15
31051 Follina
ITALY
Tel. 39 0 438 970 277
info@prealpi.it
www.prealpi.it

MÖLER DESIGN
Residenzstrasse 16
32657 Lemgo
GERMANY
Tel. 49 526 198 595
Fax. 49 526 189 218
info@moeller-design.de
www.moeller-design.de

MOLTENI & C (See ARCAYA
EQUIP, agents in Spain)
Via Rossini 50
20034 Giussano (MI)
ITALY
Tel. 39 03 623 59.1
Fax. 39 362 354 448
customer.service@molteni.it
www.molteni.it

MOON FIREWORK
Postfach 1521
635556 Gelnhausen
GERMANY
Tel. 49 6 051 470 287
Fax. 49 6 051 470 288
moonfirework@t-online.de
www.moonfirework.de

NOLTE
Konrad-Nolte-Str. 20
76726 Germersheim
GERMANY
Tel. 49 0 727 451-0
Fax. 49 0 727 451-477
www.nolte-germersheim.de

ORGANICA-ON - JOSÉ ESPINOSA
MUEBLES S.L.
Tel. 34 926 861 225
Fax. 34 926 861 225
info@organica-on.com

ONE - WUSTLICH-DESIGN AG
Carl-Friedrich-GauB-Strasse 64
47475 Kamp-Lintfort
GERMANY
Tel. 49 028 429 099 208
Fax. 49 028 429 099 225
www.wustlich-design.com

ORIZZONTI
Via Birago 12
20020 Misinto (MI)
ITALY
Tel. 39 02 966 94.1
Fax. 39 0 296 720 444
orizzonti@orizzonti-srl.com
www.orizzonti-srl.com

OSTER MÖBELWERKSTÄTTEN
Gewerbegebiet zur Höhe 1
56809 Dohr
GERMANY
Tel. 49 267 160 000

Fax. 49 2 671 600 090
moebelwerkstaetten@oster.de
www.oster.de

P2 ARCHDESIGN (Estudio de diseño)
Auf der Bünte 1
34130 Kassel
GERMANY
Tel. 49 05 616 025 858
Fax. 49 01 739 118 617
info@p2-archdesign.de
www.p2-archdesign.de

PALLUCCO ITALIA - BELLATO
Via Azzi 36
31040 Castagnole di Paese Treviso
Tel. 0422 438 500
Fax. 0422 438955
infobellato@palluccobellato.it
www.palluccobellato.it

PEROBELL
Avenida Arraona, 23
08205 Sabadell
SPAIN
Tel. 34 937 457 900
Fax. 34 7 271 500
info@perobell.com
www.perobell.com

PHILIPP PLEIN
Hebelstrasse 2
90491 Nürnberg
GERMANY
service@philipp-plein.com
www.philipp-plein.com

POLIFORM
Via Monte Santo 28
22044 Inverigo (COMO)
ITALY
Tel. 39 0 316 951
Fax. 39 031 699 444
info.poliform@poliform.it
www.poliform.it

POLTRONA FRAU
S.S. 77 Km 14,500
62029 Tolentino
ITALY
Tel. 39 07 339 090
Fax. 39 0 733 971 600
info@poltronafrau.it
www.poltronafrau.it

PORRO INDUSTRIA MOBILI
Via per Cantù 35
22060 Montesolaro (Como)
ITALY
Tel. 39 031 780 237
Fax. 39 031 781 529
info@porro.com
www.porro.com

PRESOTTO INDUSTRIE MOBILI
Via Puja, 7 fraz. Maron
33070 Brugnera (PN)
ITALY
Tel. 39 0 434 612 311
Fax. 39 0 434 621 282
pr_info@presotto.com
www.casa-design.it

PROMEMORIA
Via Montenapoleone 8
20121 Milano
ITALY
Tel. 39 0 276 000 785
info@promemoria.com
www.promemoria.com

PRO SEDA
Am Lindenbach 1
96515 Sonnebarg
GERMANY
Tel. 49 0 367 542 420
Fax. 49 03 675 424 242
info@proseda.de
www.proseda.de

RAFEMAR
Apto. De correos 98
08240 Manresa
SPAIN
rafemar@rafemar.com
www.rafemar.com

REDAELLI
Via Brianza 4
22040 Lurago d'Erba (Como)
ITALY
Tel. 39 31 607 336
Fax. 39 31 699185
REDAELLI@IVANOREDAELLI.IT
www.ivanoredaelli.com

RÖ
Sägeweg 11
CH-3073 Gümligen
SWITZERLAND
Tel. 31 9 502 140
Fax. 31 9 502 149
kollektion@roethlisberger.ch
www.roethlisberger.ch

ROSET MÖBEL GMBH (LIGNE RO-
SET in Germany)
Postfach 1230
79191 Gundelfingen/Freiburg
GERMANY
Tel. 49 761 592 090

ROSSI DI ALBIZZATE
Via Mazzini, 1
Casella postale 59
21041 Albizzate (Varese)
ITALY
Tel. 39 0 331 993 200
Fax. 39 0 331 991 583
info@rossidialbizzate.it
www.rossidialbizzate.it

RUHE RAUM
www.ruhe-raum.de

SANTA & COLE (EDICIONES DE
DISEÑO)
Santísima Trinidad del Monte 10
08017 Barcelona
SPAIN
Tel. 34 934 183 396
Fax. 34 934 183 812
www.santacole.com

SAWAYA & MORONI
Via Andegari, 18
20121 Milán
ITALY
Tel. 39 02 86 395.1
Fax. 39 02 86 39 5212 – 200
info@sawayamoroni.com
www.sawayamoroni.com

SEEFELDER
Banhofstr. 8
82229 Seefeld-Hechendorf
GERMANY
Tel. 49 0 815 299 000
Fax. 49 08 152 990 099
smw@seefelder.com
www.seefelder.com

THE WHITE COMPANY
Unit 30, Perivale Industrial Park, Hor-
senden Lane South
UB6 7RJ Greenford, Middlesex
UNITED KINGDOM
Tel. 44 08 709 009 555
Fax. 44 08 709 009 556
orders@thewhiteco.com
www.thewhiteco.com

THUT MÖBEL
CH 5103 Möriken
SWITZERLAND
Tel. 41 628 931 284
Fax. 41 628 931 110
info@thutundknup.com
www.thut.ch

TISETTANTA (Ver MIXEL.)

VERARDO
Via Pordenone, 28
33070 Tamai (Pordenone)
ITALY
Tel. 39 0 434 600 311
Fax. 39 0 434 627 155
info@verardoitalia.it

VINÇON
Passeig de Gràcia 96
08008 Barcelona
SPAIN
Tel. 34 932 156 050
Fax. 34 932 155 037
Barcelona: bcn@vincon.com
Madrid: mad@vincon.com
www.vincon.com

VITTORIO BONACINA
Via Madonnina 12
22040 Lurago d'Erba (CO)
ITALY
Tel. 39 031 699 800
Fax. 39 031 699 215
bonacina@bonacinavittorio.it
www.bonacinavittorio.it

WITTMANN
A-3492 Etsdorf/Kamp
AUSTRIA
Tel. 43 02 735 287 143
Fax. 43 027 352 877
info@wittmann.at
www.wittmann.at

WUSTLICH-DESIGN AG (Ver ONE)

ZALF - GRUPPO EUROMOBIL
Via Marosticana, 9
31010 Maser (TV)
ITALY
Tel. 39 04 239 255
Fax. 39 0 423 565 866
www.gruppoeuromobil.com

ZANOTTA
Via Vittorio Veneto 57
20054 Nova Milanese
ITALY
Tel. 39 03 624 981
Fax. 39 0 362 451 038
zanottaspa@zanotta.it
www.zanotta.it

ZEITRAUM
www.zeitraum-moebel.de